Growing up God's way
for girls

By Dr. Chris Richards and Dr. Liz Jones

EP BOOKS (Evangelical Press)
1st Floor Venture House
6 Silver Court
Watchmead
Welwyn Garden City
UK
AL7 1TS

www.epbooks.org
sales@epbooks.org

EP BOOKS are distributed in the USA by:
JPL Fulfillment
3741 Linden Avenue Southeast,
Grand Rapids, MI 49548.

E-mail: sales@jplbooks.com

First published 2013

British Library Cataloguing in Publication Data available
ISBN: 9781783970001

Unless otherwise indicated, all Scripture quotations are from the Holy Bible, English Standard Version, published by HarperCollins Publishers © 2001 by Crossway Bibles, a division of Good News Publishers. Used by permission. All rights reserved.

Published by EP Books in association with Lovewise
The two authors are trustees of the charity Lovewise, set up in 2002 to promote Christian teaching about marriage and relationships in schools and church youth groups.
www.lovewise.org.uk

Dr. Chris Richards is a Consultant Paediatrician in Newcastle upon Tyne. He is married and has five children. He is a deacon at Gateshead Presbyterian Church.

Dr. Liz Jones is a retired Community Paediatrician. She is married with three married daughters and nine grandchildren. With her husband, she attends Welbeck Road Evangelical Church, Newcastle upon Tyne.

Contents

Chapter 1
An introduction to puberty

If you look around when you are out and about, you will see that there are people in many different stages of life. There are newborn babies in prams, toddlers in buggies, children on their way to school, adults driving to work and older people out for a short walk.

A king called Solomon saw these stages of life – he called them 'seasons' – and described them in a book of the Bible called Ecclesiastes:

For everything there is a season, and a time for every matter under heaven.

Ecclesiastes 3:1

During puberty young people move from one stage of life to another, as they leave childhood and move on their way towards becoming an adult. Puberty is a time of big changes to your body and mind. The changes are fast. Except as a newborn baby, there is no other time when you will grow as rapidly as you do during puberty. The changes are also big – both to your body (affecting its size, shape and nature) and to your mind (affecting how you understand things and make choices and plans for the future).

Growing up is God's idea

In thinking about the changes ahead, it is good to remember the following things.

O These changes are part of God's design for you

In His wisdom, God did not suddenly throw any of us into life as an adult; rather, He arranged it that we would grow into the role. Even Jesus, God's own Son, experienced these changes in His life as He 'increased in wisdom and in stature' (Luke 2:52).

○ The timing of these changes is under God's control

God gives a baby his first teeth at about 6 months, just when the baby needs to move from a diet of mainly milk to a diet of mainly solid food. In the same way, the changes that God causes to happen in your body during puberty remind us just how good and wise He is. These changes are out of your control; but wait patiently and you will see that the results will be of great benefit to you.

○ God promises to lead his people through all the stages of their lives

God knows everything that we go through and every change that happens to our bodies before it happens and in precise detail! King David knew of God's safe and steady hand on his life, even in the most challenging of circumstances, and so could say:

> But I trust in you, O LORD;
> I say, "You are my God."
> My times are in your hand.
>
> Psalm 31:14,15

○ Parents will help you through this stage of your life

You may be reading this book with one or both of your parents. God has given your parents a special responsibility to guide and help you through this exciting and demanding time. Remember to talk to them and listen to their advice!

○ The changes have a God-given purpose

The changes of puberty are designed by God to prepare you for the future.

Puberty is designed to bring you to adulthood so that you can live independently of your parents and so that one day you may be able to have a family of your own.

The changes of puberty will allow you to live for God in new ways as you have the exciting prospect of taking on new roles, meeting new people and seeing more of the world.

You are not ready... yet

Right now, you would not be able to set up home and have a family if you wanted to. There are several reasons for this:

O There are *emotional* reasons. You just do not feel ready! You may wisely feel that you still need the advice, regular care and protection of your parents.

O There are *physical* reasons. Your body is not yet mature enough to have children.

O There are *spiritual* reasons. You are not ready to face all the temptations and difficulties that come with adult responsibilities.

O There are *legal* reasons. The law of most countries recognises the factors that we have just outlined and wisely makes it impossible for children to live independently of their parents or guardians. It is not possible to marry until the age of 16 in the UK and in many US states and, even then, only with the permission of your parents.

The changes that occur between now and the end of puberty will allow you to grow up, live independently and have a family of your own. Here are just three aspects of these changes:

1. You will develop new desires and feelings... so that you are attracted to the opposite sex.

2. You will change physically... so that you may have children.

3. You will grow in maturity... so that you can make responsible decisions.

The challenge of change

Important as these changes are, your most important challenge is to make wise choices. Your growing and maturing body and mind will allow you to do new and different things. You will have to decide whether you are going to do these things in the right way or the wrong way.

These are called *moral choices*. You will need to ask God to help you to make the right decisions when faced with these new moral choices. You must prepare yourself to think and act with your new adult abilities and responsibilities in a way that pleases God.

In this book we want to help you to learn about the changes in your body and mind that will happen during puberty. We also want to equip you to make good decisions that will please God as you get older.

Chapter 2
Marriage

Why learn about marriage?

In His wisdom God has given us one basic design for forming a family; this design is based on marriage. Over the next few years you will make decisions that might affect whether it will be possible for you to have a family in the way God intends. You will need to think and act in a way that pleases God and not do anything that might spoil this opportunity.

For these reasons, it is important to learn about marriage now, even though actually getting married may seem a long way off.

Marriage - a special design

Have you ever seen a wedding? Did everyone seem very happy? Was there an exciting atmosphere? Yes, it is obvious to anyone at a wedding that it is a very special occasion. But this is not only because of the dress, confetti and cake; at a wedding the couple show their love for each other by starting the life-long relationship of marriage.

Marriage was designed by God. The first man and woman created by God, Adam and Eve, were also husband and wife, setting a pattern for men and women to follow in the future. These words from the first book of the Bible called Genesis show that this was God's intention:

For this reason a man will leave his father and mother and be united to his wife, and they will become one flesh.

Genesis 2:24 (NIV)

This is why marriage is known as a *creation ordinance*. A creation ordinance is an arrangement, designed by God, which has been present since the creation of the world. Marriage is recorded throughout history and in all the nations around the world, even by people who do not recognise God as its designer.

Marriage has been designed to be the basis of each family unit, so that children can be born into a family and benefit from the love and security of family life. This is the way that God has chosen to raise one generation after another to work and care for His world and so fulfil God's command to 'be fruitful and multiply and fill the earth and subdue it' (Genesis 1:28). Just as a building is made up of individual bricks, so God intends all nations and their communities to be made up of the building bricks of the family unit based on marriage. Without strong marriages, a country stops working properly and starts to fall apart.

Once we realise that God is the designer of marriage, is it any wonder that we get excited about a wedding when we see His design put into practice as a new family forms and a new unit of society takes shape?

Who can get married?

We can find the answer to this question by looking at God's own description of marriage in the verse which we have just read: 'a man will leave his father and mother and be united to his wife, and they will become one flesh' (Genesis 2:24 [NIV]).

From this, we learn that God designed marriage to be between a man and a woman. God has designed a man and a woman to be different – not only in their bodies, but also in how they feel and the way they think.

The differences between a man and woman allow them to take on different roles in marriage. God designed Eve to be Adam's helper and companion. It is God's intention that both the husband and the wife work together in a *complementary* way so that both they and their children benefit.

To complement means to act together in different ways for the good of both. As the head of the family, the husband should take the lead in providing for it, in protecting it from threats and in teaching his children. The wife should support her husband in these responsibilities, and take a greater part in running the home, and in feeding and caring for the family.

We also learn from this verse (Genesis 2:24) that God intends that there should be only *one* husband ('a man') and *one* wife ('his wife'). In addition, we observe that Adam and Eve were adults when they married. God intends marriage to be for those who have been through puberty, so that they are mature in the way they think and old enough to have children.

Leaving and uniting

The same verse shows other things about marriage as well. It states that, when a man marries, he is to 'leave his father and mother'. You might have noticed that, at a wedding, the bride walks in with her father and then walks out with her new husband. This represents an important part of getting married. The husband and wife must leave their parents and join together to form a new family as a married couple.

We also learn that when a man and a woman get married, they are 'united' in many important ways. They live together and share everything: food, money, surname, holidays... They share their thoughts in making decisions together. They also unite their bodies in special physical closeness, which the Bible describes as the two becoming 'one flesh'.

The order in which we do things is very important to God. In Genesis 2:24, the *leaving* of the family home is followed by *uniting* in marriage, which in turn is followed by the *two becoming one flesh*.

Today, many people in our society are choosing to go against this God-given order. Most commonly, they unite their bodies without getting married first. Others try to form a new family home before they have properly left their parents' home. Ignoring God's order in this way can lead to all kinds of problems.

The promises of marriage

Marriage is based on the promises that are made between a husband (bridegroom) and his wife (bride) on their wedding day. The bride and bridegroom usually give rings to each other and they wear these for the rest of their lives to remind them of the promises they have made. Because a ring does not have an end, it is a good example of the unending love between a husband and a wife.

These promises of marriage are very serious and are made before God and those present at the wedding; they are sometimes called 'vows'. A promise is the act of saying what you intend to do and then doing everything in your power to carry it out. When God makes a promise to His people, He always keeps it. This is a mark of His faithfulness to us. Similarly, God requires us to keep our promises. In fact, a Christian should be known as one who keeps her promises, even when it hurts her to do so (see Psalm 15:4). To say one thing but do another is one form of lying, which is forbidden by God in the ninth of the Ten Commandments, 'You shall not bear false witness against your neighbour' (Exodus 20:16). It is, therefore, important to think very seriously before making the promises of marriage.

Here is one version of the marriage vows spoken by the bride:

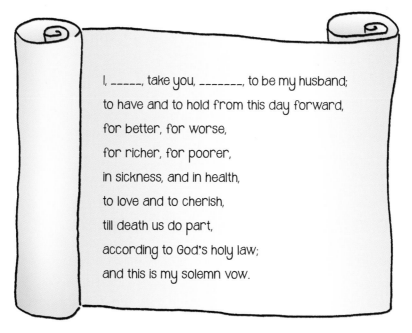

I, _____, take you, _____, to be my husband;

to have and to hold from this day forward,

for better, for worse,

for richer, for poorer,

in sickness, and in health,

to love and to cherish,

till death us do part,

according to God's holy law;

and this is my solemn vow.

The words of the vows express the love that the bride and bridegroom have for each other. Note the word *cherish*, which is not a common word nowadays. To cherish means to show your appreciation for someone of great value to you. A husband and wife cherish each other by taking great care to seek the very best for each other.

These qualities of love are described in the following Bible passage, which is often read out at weddings:

> Love is patient and kind; love does not envy or boast; it is not arrogant or rude. It does not insist on its own way; it is not irritable or resentful; it does not rejoice at wrongdoing, but rejoices with the truth. Love bears all things, believes all things, hopes all things, endures all things. Love never ends.
>
> 1 Corinthians 13:4-8

This is the kind of love that the husband and wife are promising to share with each other when they make their vows.

More about love in marriage

The Bible gives us two special descriptions of how a husband should love his wife. He should do so in the same way that Christ loves His church and gave His life for the church (Ephesians 5:25). He should also love his wife as his own body (Ephesians 5:28). In other words, the husband should look after his wife just as he looks after himself. What a challenge! Boys need to think about this carefully. It is not easy for them to be a husband as God intends.

The demands of marriage are equally challenging for the wife. She needs to be prepared to respect and submit to her husband (Ephesians 5:22) – so you need to think carefully whether you are prepared to do this for the man you plan to marry.

Note that there are no 'ifs' or 'buts' in the vows of marriage. You promise to be devoted to your husband, whatever circumstances develop. This is sometimes called *unconditional love*. You may marry a millionaire or an athlete, but you have promised to be faithful to your husband, even if all the money runs out or he ends up in a wheelchair.

This kind of love is a *decision* to love the other person, so is not ultimately dependent on your feelings or what happens in the marriage. You simply promise to put the other person's interests before your own. This is very different from the kind of love that we often hear about on the television or read about in magazines, where people are often seen marrying and breaking up a few years later.

Finally, the words 'till death us do part' in the marriage vows are very important. God intends marriage to be life-long, only ending with the death of the husband or wife.

What are God's purposes for marriage?

The first should be obvious from what has been said about love in marriage. The husband and wife must love, care for and support each other. So your husband should be your very best friend for life.

The second purpose for marriage is to have children. It is God's intention that children should benefit from being born and brought up in a family based on the security of marriage.

A plant grows best when it has adequate amounts of water, food and sun. We know from studies that children do best in a married family.[1] Can you think of some of the reasons why a secure and happy marriage helps a child? Remember the marriage vows. Think of the strength and help that children receive from knowing that they have a mother and father who have promised to keep on loving each other whatever happens.

For several reasons, not all children are part of a married family, but whatever your circumstances, you can trust in God who promises to care for us.

---

1 See, for example, 'Why marriage matters: Thirty conclusions from social sciences' published in 2012 by Institute of American Values, available on-line from www.americanvalues.org

Chapter 3
Puberty and how it starts

Do you remember what you read about puberty in the first chapter? Puberty is a stage of life which involves big changes to your mind and body that prepare you to be an adult. As an adult, you will be able to live independently of your parents, get married and have a family.

Boys and girls - similar but different!

Before we look at the details, let us remember that when God created the world, He made human beings 'in His own image' (Genesis 1:27). For this reason, both men and women have important things in common. They are both equally valuable to God. They both have a God-given conscience to distinguish right from wrong. Recognising this, we should not be surprised that some of the changes of puberty are similar in boys and girls. Both can expect to increase rapidly in height and to change in body shape. Both mature not only in their bodies, but also in their minds.

But God also created human beings to be 'male and female' (Genesis 1:27). For this reason, men and women are distinctively different. We have already seen how men and women have different roles in marriage. Not surprisingly then, their preparation for adult life is somewhat different – there are important differences between the changes of puberty in boys and girls. Of course, these differences do not begin at puberty – anyone who has changed a baby's nappy will see this!

God has designed the changes of puberty to allow a woman to do things in raising a family that no man can do – to become pregnant, to give birth to a child and to breastfeed the child in the first few months of his life. The obvious differences between men and women in size and body shape are reflected by substantial differences inside the body. Women have different *hormones* (see pages 31 and 44) from men and the levels of a woman's hormones go up and down at different times of the month, whilst a man's hormones are very steady.

The changes that take place in the mind during puberty mean that men and women also think differently. For example they are different in what makes them pleased or anxious, or how they view a problem. Generally, women tend to be more sensitive than men and consider it to be very important how they get on with someone. Men are often physically stronger and may be better at logically analysing problems.[2]

Men and women are even different in what tempts them to sin. The Bible warns women about gossiping (1 Timothy 5:13), whilst it warns men about not picking fights with each other (1 Timothy 2:8)!

The differences between men and women work well in a marriage. We have already described in Chapter 2 how the husband and wife have been designed by God to complement each other. Men have been designed to take the lead and provide for a family, whilst women have been

2 See Chapters 3-6 of 'The Essential Difference' by Simon Baron-Cohen published by Penguin 2003

designed to nurture and care for it. We live in a society which pretends that these differences do not exist, but it actually damages both men and women, as well as our society, when we try to hide the truth about these differences.

How does it all start?

Between the ages of 9 and 11 in girls and 10 and 13 in boys, things begin to change. This will happen at different times in different people. Do not worry if your friends have started puberty and you have not. The changes do not take place all at once but over a number of years, so puberty may not end until you are 15 or 16.

Interesting Fact

On average, girls go through puberty about one year earlier than boys. This is one reason why many girls will become taller than boys of the same age for a time, before the boys catch up and usually overtake them.

Puberty starts when your brain begins to cause the release of certain chemicals, called *hormones*, into your blood stream. Hormones can be described as chemical messengers – their role is to transmit a message from one part of the body to another. These hormones then wake up and change various special parts of the body – different parts and in different ways for boys and girls.

How the changes of puberty take place is amazingly complicated and much of it remains a mystery. Perhaps it can be compared to an army. The Commander-in-Chief is in ultimate control of all his men through the leadership of his officers, who in turn control the different types of soldier – foot soldiers, artillerymen and engineers. In order that the whole army can work together in a co-ordinated attack, the Commander-in-Chief needs two things: a sure way of communicating, whether by radio or more modern technology; and a clear chain of command. The Commander-in-Chief informs his officers so that they know his exact plans at every stage of the campaign. His officers then spread the message on the ground so that all the soldiers know what is required of them.

God has chosen a part of the brain called the hypothalamus to act as a Commander-in-Chief by starting off and then controlling the process of growing up. The chain of command (see diagram on opposite page) runs from your hypothalamus to the pituitary gland, which is also in the brain, and this sends two different hormones into the bloodstream. These hormones are called Luteinising Hormone and Follicle Stimulating Hormone, or LH and FSH for short. With these hormones the brain communicates with the cells of the ovaries in girls (and testicles in boys). The ovaries, situated in your lower tummy, will then start to produce two other hormones called oestrogen and progesterone. When this happens, you will start to notice the first changes of puberty in your body.

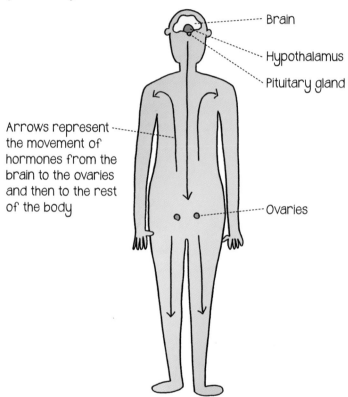

Brain

Hypothalamus

Pituitary gland

Arrows represent the movement of hormones from the brain to the ovaries and then to the rest of the body

Ovaries

Interesting fact

The age that a child begins puberty has got earlier and earlier in the last 160 years – by about two and a half years. Scientists are not sure why this is, though better food may be one reason.

Chapter 4
How your body changes

We start this section with a warning to be careful how you think and talk when we consider these changes. We need to refer to certain special parts of the body – parts that the apostle Paul refers to as 'unpresentable' (1 Corinthians 12:23). By this he means that they are parts that we normally choose to keep private and cover with our clothes. The verse tells us that we need to treat these parts with special 'modesty'. That means that we must be careful only to talk about these things in a right and respectful way.

Before we say more about how the girl's body changes in puberty, have a look at the diagram below which shows the parts of the body that allow a woman to have a baby (reproductive organs). Most of these are hidden inside the lower tummy.

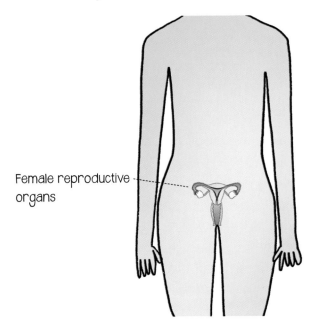

Female reproductive organs

A closer look...

With the help of the diagram below, identify the following parts of the body, which are in **bold**:

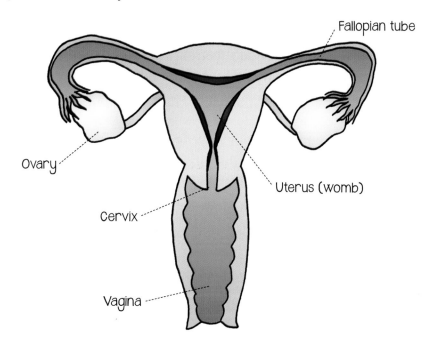

The two **ovaries** are the site of female egg production. The ovary also produces the two female hormones called *oestrogen* and *progesterone*. Oestrogen causes many of the important changes of puberty – those *inside* the body that will allow her to have a baby as well as the *outward* changes, such as breast development that will allow her to feed her baby. Progesterone causes the lining of the uterus (womb) to thicken in preparation for pregnancy.

The **uterus** is also known as the 'womb'. This is the place where a baby develops until he is ready to be born.

The **fallopian tube** connects the ovary to the uterus.

The **cervix** is the entrance to the womb and separates it from the vagina. It is usually very narrow, but opens wide to allow a baby to be born.

The **vagina** is also known as the birth canal. This is where the reproductive organs open to the outside of the body.

Having identified some important parts of a girl's body, we are now ready to examine some of the changes that take place in her body during puberty.

Change one - the menstrual cycle begins

As well as bringing on the changes of puberty, the female hormones, oestrogen and progesterone, also control the process which God has designed to allow a woman to have a baby. This process involves the rise and fall of these hormones in a woman's body in an approximately 28-day pattern called the *menstrual cycle*. Unless a woman becomes pregnant, each of these cycles will involve a loss of blood from her vagina; this is called a *period*. Most young women start to have periods by 14 years of age.

Below is a wheel of days that represents a complete 28-day (monthly) menstrual cycle. The 5-day period (bleeding) is shown in pink. The 5 days of fertility (the time when she is able to become pregnant) are shown in green. This time of fertility is usually just before halfway through the monthly cycle. Work your way clockwise round the wheel, noting the different phases.

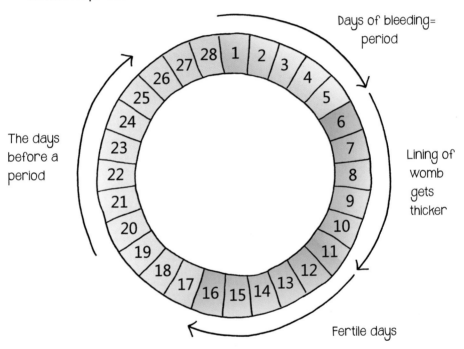

Days of bleeding= period

The days before a period

Lining of womb gets thicker

Fertile days

To understand why a woman has a period, let us follow an egg's journey from the ovary down the reproductive tract (see the opposite page). Usually during each menstrual cycle, a single egg leaves one of the ovaries and travels down the fallopian tube towards the womb.

The egg's journey

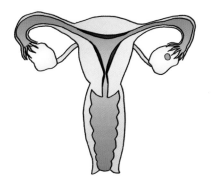

The egg is stored in the ovary before release.

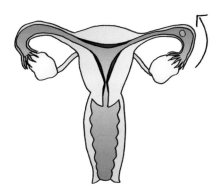

The egg is released into the fallopian tube.

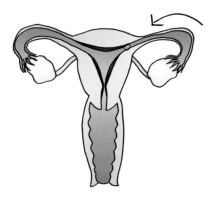

The egg moves down the fallopian tube towards the womb, where the lining has been thickened with blood to receive an embryo if pregnancy occurs.

There are only *two* possible outcomes of each menstrual cycle, depending on what happens:

○ Outcome one - the start of pregnancy

A woman becomes pregnant if her egg is fertilised by a sperm (the male equivalent of eggs). *Fertilisation* is the joining of a sperm and an egg to form one cell and this marks the start of a new life. At this very early stage the baby is sometimes called an *embryo*. We shall learn more about how this happens in the next chapter.

○ Outcome two - a period

If, as is usually the case, fertilisation of the egg does not happen, then the amount of the hormone progesterone in a woman's body starts to fall. Because progesterone maintains the lining of the womb, this then comes away from the inside of the womb and passes out of the body through the woman's vagina, together with the remains of the unfertilised egg. This is a woman's *period*.

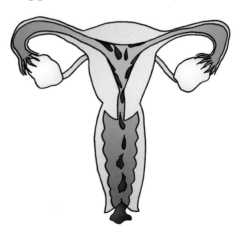

Practical information about periods

During the few days before and during a period, a girl may feel some pain low down in her tummy. Before a period, she may also become tearful and easily upset. This is sometimes called *'pre-menstrual tension'* or PMT for short. The emotional changes are caused by the changes in hormone levels. You may need some mild painkillers if you have a tummy pain just before and during your period.

During your period, you will need to use a pad (sanitary towel) in your underwear or a tampon to prevent blood leaking onto your clothes. Your mother will help you buy these.

Pads will need to be changed regularly, especially when the period is heaviest (usually the second or third day after the start of bleeding). There are thicker pads for use at night. During your period, you will want to take a shower or bath more often.

Girls tend to use tampons instead of pads when they get older and once they feel happy about inserting them into the vagina. The advantage of wearing a tampon is that it allows women to go swimming and play sport without the period stopping them.

It can be difficult to learn how to use a tampon but here are two important tips:

1 Only try to put in a tampon when you are bleeding enough for the blood to act as a lubricant; this makes the insertion more comfortable.

2 Most girls imagine that they need to put in the tampon aiming towards their head. From the diagram below you can see that the direction is really towards the middle of the back.

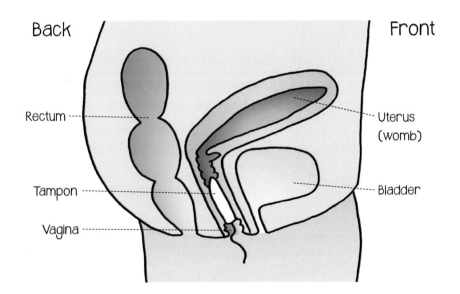

Back   Front

Rectum

Uterus (womb)

Tampon

Bladder

Vagina

Change two - breast enlargement

The changes in the breasts are the earliest signs of puberty in a girl. Throughout puberty, the breasts will gradually get bigger. The development of the breasts is one way that God prepares the woman's body for future responsibilities as a mother.

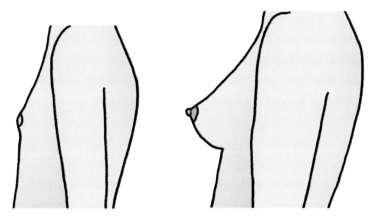

In order to be comfortable, you will need to buy bras of the right size once these changes are underway. The final breast size varies greatly between one woman and another.

Change three - standing tall

An adult is taller and bigger than you are! This is caused in part by the effect of hormones that make bones longer and muscles bigger. During the next few years, you will shoot up fast. You will notice that you grow out of your clothes very quickly as you move through puberty.

Change four - hair in new places

Under the influence of your hormones, you will develop hair in your armpits and in your *genital area* (the triangular area between your legs and around the entrance of your vagina). You may also notice more hair on your legs.

Together with this increased hair growth, especially in your armpits, you will notice that you sweat more. This will be the time to start washing more often and to use a deodorant, either in the form of a roll-on or a spray. Some girls also start to shave their legs and armpits during puberty.

Change five - annoying spots

Not all the effects of your hormones are welcome. Acne is a skin condition of the face (and sometimes the back and shoulders) that affects some people during puberty. It consists of small red spots, sometimes with pus in the centre, especially around the chin and nose. If it is severe, your doctor may be able to prescribe a cream or tablet to treat the spots. The good news is that acne tends to improve towards the end of puberty.

Chapter 5
How the body changes in boys

Here are a few of the important changes that occur in boys during puberty.

Change one - the genital area

A man's genital area contains the reproductive organs including the penis, testicles and scrotum (see diagram below), which allow him to become a father. Note that, unlike in a woman, these organs are on the outside of the body.

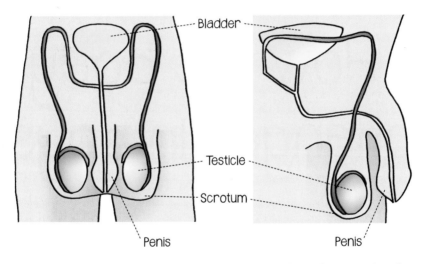

In a boy, the first sign that puberty has begun is the enlargement of his testicles caused by the effects of the hormones LH and FSH. The testicles are two round balls that hang down behind a man's penis. The testicles enlarge because of the development inside them of two types of cell which produce two different and important things. One type makes sperm – these are the male equivalent of eggs but with a tail. The other type causes the release of *testosterone* – the most important male hormone.

Testosterone produces many of the changes of puberty in a boy's body. These include the enlargement of the penis and thickening of the scrotum around the testicles, as well as the changes to the voice and the hair growth described below.

Interesting fact

For sperm to grow in a healthy way, the testicles need to be cooler than body temperature (just by a degree or two). For this reason, God has designed the testicles to lie in a sac outside the body called the scrotum.

Change two - speaking deeply

The sound of our voice is caused by the vibration of our vocal cords. During puberty in a boy, testosterone makes the voice box grow and the vocal cords lengthen. If you play a stringed instrument, you will know that the longer the string, the lower the note that is formed. In the same way, the lengthening of the vocal cords causes a boy's voice to deepen. This is described as his voice *breaking*.

We might want to ask ourselves why God has given a man a deeper voice than a child or woman? It may be that a deep voice suits many of the demands of a man's role as leader of a church or his family. The 18th century preachers John Wesley and George Whitefield preached to tens of thousands of people at a time in the open air without a microphone!

Interesting fact

The man's voice is about one octave lower than that of a woman. This allows men and women to sing in harmony. This is an example of how God designed men and women to work together to create something beautiful.

Change three - hair in new places

Under the influence of testosterone, hair starts to grow in the beard area. Unless they plan to grow a beard, young men will have to start shaving at this stage. Young men also start to grow hair in the armpits and genital area during puberty. The presence of hair on the face and other places, together with a bigger jaw which also grows during puberty, are further God-given features that distinguish men from women.

Chapter 6
Physical intimacy

A special gift for a special time

In chapter two we learned that the husband and wife are described in the Bible as two becoming 'one flesh'. They experience this unity in many ways in their marriage as they live together and share everything. One of the ways that this unity is expressed is through physical intimacy (closeness). They show their love by kissing and hugging each other and by sharing their bodies in  sexual intercourse (sometimes called *making love*).

Physical intimacy between a husband and wife is a close and private matter. Even when we think about this subject, we need to be very careful to honour God in our thoughts. We have already seen how the Bible tells us that we need to treat the parts of our body involved in intimacy with special modesty. We must be careful only to talk about these things in a right and respectful way – and not to allow the wrong sort of emotions or desires to be stirred up in our heads.

It is because of this need for modesty, that God has made us tend to feel embarrassed when we think about these things

– perhaps you are aware of this as you read this chapter. Such feelings may make you uncomfortable, but they are actually helpful in protecting you against wrong thoughts and interests.

Here are some details about how the married couple show their love in sexual intercourse. After a time of physical closeness and enjoyment between the husband and wife, the husband gently slides his penis, which has become stiff, into his wife's vagina. We may note how God has designed the man's penis to fit into the woman's vagina. This reminds us that sexual intercourse was designed by God to be between a man and a woman.

After a few minutes, at a special moment, some fluid containing millions of sperm passes out of the husband's body into his wife's body, in a process called *ejaculation*. Sperm have a tail which allows them to swim from the vagina through the cervix to the womb and fallopian tubes. If sexual intercourse occurs at the fertile time in the menstrual cycle, when the egg has been released from the wife's ovary, one of the husband's sperm may meet and join with his wife's egg in an event called *fertilisation*. In this way, the wife becomes pregnant. A new life has begun! The Bible describes this event as the mother *conceiving* her child.

The process of fertilisation

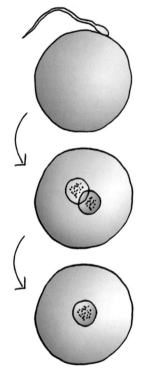

The sperm is about to enter the woman's egg, it does this by burrowing through the surface.

Then the genes from the husband's sperm and the wife's egg start to join together.

Once the genes have joined together, they create a new cell, which is called an embryo. A new life has now begun!

Only one sperm can fertilise a female egg to form an embryo, because once fertilisation occurs, the surface of the embryo changes to stop any other sperm from joining with it. This ensures that the new baby develops from just the right genes – from one and not from two or more sperm.

Genes are the chemicals which contain the code of information that allows the cells of the body to work and which are unique to each person.

These events show us that sexual intercourse has two important purposes – which are actually the two purposes of marriage that we explained earlier. Sexual intercourse has been given by God so that the husband and wife can express their love to each other; and sometimes, out of that love, a new life is formed.

So special that God has given us rules

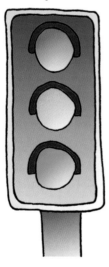

It might seem attractive to live in a world where there are no laws. (Of course it would mean that your parents would never be able to tell you that you were doing something wrong!) But have you ever thought what would happen if there were no laws about how we should drive a car? The laws of the road make it safe for us to drive. If there were none, many more people on the road would get injured and driving would be a very frightening experience.

God has given us a law regarding how we relate to the opposite sex in sexual intimacy. This law is the seventh of the Ten Commandments: 'You shall not commit adultery' (Exodus 20:14). From this verse and other passages in the Bible, we learn that all sexual activity outside marriage is wrong. The word *adultery* means either being married and experiencing sexual intimacy with someone who is not your husband, or experiencing sexual intimacy with someone else's husband. In the New Testament, God warns us to 'flee from sexual immorality' (1 Corinthians 6:18). The term 'sexual immorality' includes any sexual activity that is not between a husband and his wife.

The fact that God has given us a specific command to keep sexual intimacy for marriage shows how important God considers sexual intimacy to be. The husband and wife are important to Him, their marriage is important to Him, and the new life that may result from sexual intimacy is important to Him. God's law about sexual intimacy is for our safety and well-being – it protects us, it protects marriage, and it protects young life.

The early days of life

Fertilisation usually takes place in one of the fallopian tubes. The embryo then moves down the tube and into the uterus (womb). At this stage of the menstrual cycle, the lining of the womb is thickened, like a soft cushion, due to the action of the hormone progesterone, and is ready to receive the embryo. A few days after fertilisation, the embryo implants in (lands on and fixes to) the wall of the womb and the pregnancy continues.

The Bible describes how God is involved in forming and sustaining new life from the baby's earliest moments. You can read about this in Psalm 139: 13-16. In His wisdom, God knows exactly how the baby's new body should develop and how each of his cells should work.

The new baby develops

Very soon after fertilisation, a recognisable baby starts to develop – just a few days after the head and body form, arms and legs start to develop. Internal organs also develop at this time. Just before 4 weeks after fertilisation, the heart, the size of a poppy seed (0.5mm diameter), starts to beat

for the first time. By 10 weeks after fertilisation, the baby, who is about 5.5cm long, starts to move inside the womb. Around this time, the baby also starts to suck and yawn.

Here is a photo of a baby 10 weeks after fertilisation. The baby is only 5.5cm long. Can you see his/her ear, nose, hands, elbow and knees?

During his time in the womb, the baby does not breathe oxygen through his lungs or take food into his mouth (although he can take gulps of the amniotic fluid that surrounds him). Instead, all his food and oxygen come to him from his mother's blood stream through the placenta and umbilical cord (see diagram).

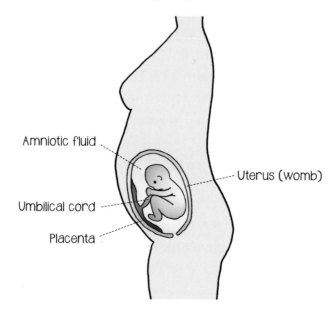

Amniotic fluid

Uterus (womb)

Umbilical cord

Placenta

About half way through her pregnancy (18-20 weeks), the mother starts to feel the baby kicking.

The baby gets ready to be born

Finally, after 9 months (40 weeks) of pregnancy, the baby has grown enough and is ready to be born – that exciting day when the parents meet their baby face-to-face for the first time.

The mother gives birth in a process called *labour*, which is controlled by hormones. The thick muscular wall of the womb starts to contract strongly (labour pains), opening the cervix and gradually pushing the baby out of the womb over a period of several hours. The baby is now mature enough to live outside the mother – although even after birth the baby is totally dependent on the mother for warmth, food and protection.

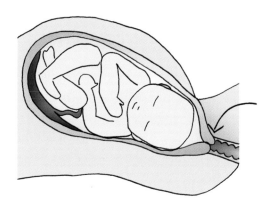

Before the mother goes into labour, the cervix is still closed.

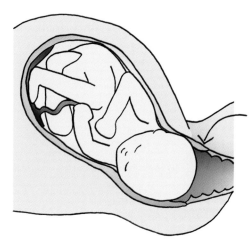

The cervix is now fully open and the baby's head is being pushed down by contractions.

Interesting Fact

In about one in every 80 natural pregnancies, twins occur. They arise from one of two circumstances. Either two eggs are released from the ovaries and each is fertilised (non-identical twins) or a fertilised embryo splits before implantation (identical twins).

When fertilisation does not occur

Though God has designed the menstrual cycle to allow a woman to become pregnant, this does not happen during each cycle. If she has not been sexually intimate in the fertile days of her menstrual cycle, then she will not become pregnant. In this case, levels of the hormone progesterone, which maintains the lining of the womb, start to fall. The lining then comes away from the inside of the womb and passes out of the body together with the remains of the unfertilised egg. This process causes bleeding from the woman's vagina known as a *period* (or *menstruation*).

Chapter 7
Changes in the way you think

Do you remember how we explained that the changes of puberty affect your mind as well as your body? Here are three important ways in which you will think differently as a result of puberty.

Change one - growing in maturity

What would you think if you saw a child driving a public bus down the street? 'That is not safe! He is just too young to be driving!' You would be right to be concerned because his mind is too immature to cope with the decisions and responsibilities of such a job. Fortunately, during puberty your *mind* will mature as well as your body so that you will be ready to handle your new adult responsibilities. Growing up takes a long time – God has given you nearly twenty years to prepare you to think in an adult way.

In the Bible, Paul describes the process of becoming mature in these words: 'When I was a child, I spoke like a child, I thought like a child, I reasoned like a child. When I became a man, I gave up childish ways' (1 Corinthians 13:11). Your increasing maturity of mind will affect what you say, how you think and how you feel. In fact, it will affect everything that you do!

God expects you to use this greater maturity for His glory. If you are growing up as a believing Christian, becoming mature in your mind means an increasing understanding of how to follow God's ways that are shown to us in the Bible. Rather than only thinking about yourself, you will learn to show love to others in acts of kindness and thoughtfulness (see 1 John 4:11).

Change two - feeling moody

The process of maturing in your mind is not always easy. Together with all these helpful changes may come other more awkward, and sometimes powerful, emotions which make you feel moody, sad or misunderstood, and may tempt you to become bad-tempered.

There are at least two reasons why this happens:

1 The hormone changes inside you can produce these feelings.

2 Some of the challenges ahead of you may seem stressful. For example, although you may look forward to growing up, the new responsibilities of being an adult may also concern you.

These feelings are a challenge! And they may tempt you to sin – to be unloving towards God and towards those around you. They may particularly tempt you to break the fifth of the Ten Commandments, 'Honour your father and your mother' (Exodus 20:12), by being unloving or disobedient to your parents, who love and care for you most. If you feel moody, you need to ask God for help to be loving and patient. (Your parents may need to do this as well!)

Change three - new attractions

Before puberty, you may have thought little about boys. However, this may change over the next few years. Certainly the effects of hormones will influence this. Sooner or later, you will start to be interested in boys and attracted to them in a way you have not been before.

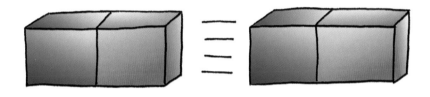

What does *attraction* mean? You might remember using the word *attraction* about magnets in a science lesson. Negative and positive ends of magnets are attracted to each other -- the ends are drawn towards each other. In a similar way, you might find yourself feeling attracted to be with a young man so that you can get to know him better. You might also be drawn to how he looks. This is sometimes called *fancying* somebody. In younger people, especially when their interest is towards an older person, this can be called a *crush*.

What are these feelings all about?

Like everything else God has made, these feelings of attraction are intended for a good purpose: to draw a man and a woman together and, perhaps eventually, to strengthen the bond between them in marriage.

Jacob in the Bible served his uncle Laban for seven years in order to earn his marriage to Rachel, but because he loved her so much, it seemed like a very short time to him (Genesis 29:20). Perhaps one day your future husband may feel like this towards you!

Three reasons for caution

You need to be very careful about these feelings of attraction for the following reasons:

1. It is important to enjoy the many things that God has given you at the moment – e.g. the opportunity to study, have lots of friends and play sport, rather than to long for things that He may give you in the future. Have you ever looked longingly at some clothes in a shop window or at the latest mobile phone that has just come onto the market? There is no point in longing for things if they are too expensive. In the same way, aim to enjoy your teenage years free from wanting things that you are not ready for.

2. Although it is not wrong to be attracted to a boy, it is easy for these feelings of attraction to get out of control, just as it is not easy to get a puppy back to sleep once you have woken him up. Uncontrolled feelings can very easily dominate your thoughts and lead you to forget about the importance of putting God first in your life and decisions.

3. These feelings of attraction might cause you to disobey God in how you relate to those of the opposite sex. In doing so, you are likely to hurt others, as well as yourself, and perhaps cause them to sin too. We shall look at this in some detail later.

Unhelpful influences

It is easy for these feelings of attraction to be stirred up by what you read and see. So much around you is aimed at encouraging them. Such feelings are a popular topic on television and in music – but remember that broadcasters and song-writers often show little or no respect for God's wisdom. Social network sites can also expose you to the thoughts and activities of those who do not follow God's ways.

Enjoy being single

The Bible says many good things about being single. It is described as a gift from God (1 Corinthians 7:7). Paul goes on to explain that there are advantages in serving God as a single person without the responsibilities of being in a relationship or caring and providing for a husband or children. God calls some of us to be single for a short time, some for the whole of our lives.

Self-control is mentioned as fruit of the Holy Spirit (Galatians 5:23). God asks us to be self-controlled about our feelings. So for now you can enjoy the company of boys, but remember to treat them with kindness and respect, and to protect your heart against any wrong desires or actions.

Chapter 8
Going out and beyond

Although the time when you might get married may seem a long way away, you may still be wondering how people get from where you are now to the point of getting married. Most people do not suddenly get married! In some cultures, parents arrange the marriages of their children, but in our culture the following are common steps to marriage from singleness.

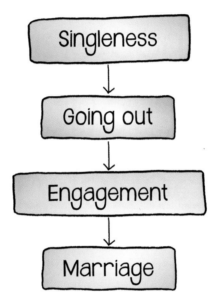

Singleness

You may spend some time being single, especially if you need to continue your education after you finish high school. But one day you may meet a young man to whom you are attracted and whom you consider a good friend. If he is attracted to you as well, then he might ask you to go out with him.

Going out

Going out (sometimes called *dating*) is a friendship between a young man and a young woman that is:

○ exclusive (you do not go out with two people at the same time)

○ committed (at least for a time)

○ public (others know about it)

So what is the purpose of going out? Does an exclusive and public relationship between a man and a woman remind you of something? Marriage! Now, going out is *not* marriage, but it has a purpose that is related to it – it is a way of getting to know each other to see if your friendship might grow and lead to the possibility of getting married one day in the future.

If it becomes clear that the person whom you are going out with is not the right person for you to marry, then it is right and proper to let them know and stop going out before either of you is too deeply hurt through disappointment.

You might go out for some months or longer before it is clear whether you are well suited and whether it would be right to get married. At this point, your boyfriend might ask you to marry him. It is also respectful and wise for your boyfriend to ask your father for his permission to marry you. If your father agrees and you are willing to get married, then you become *engaged*.

Engagement

Engagement is an agreement between a man and a woman that they plan to get married. It is the time to tell everyone about their plan. But it is not marriage itself and so it is important that they show self-control in how they feel and act towards each other during this time. God does not intend us to be sexually intimate at this stage. And it is important to realise that sometimes engagements end and do not lead to marriage.

Marriage - thinking ahead

The decision to get married has rightly been described as one of the biggest decisions of someone's life, so it needs very careful thought. This is why the marriage service includes these or similar words:

No one should enter into it lightly or selfishly but reverently and responsibly in the sight of Almighty God.

Some people rush into marriage without carefully considering whether it is wise to do so. The Bible warns us of the danger of making vows that we regret later (Proverbs 20:25). Your thoughts about whom you would like to spend the rest of your life with will probably be different in five or ten years' time!

Believers in the Lord Jesus Christ should not marry non-believers. The Bible says 'Do not be unequally yoked (coupled) with unbelievers' (2 Corinthians 6:14). The verses after this one make it clear that believers and non-believers are completely different – described as 'light and dark'. Such a marriage would be between two people with very different priorities in their lives; it is also likely to lead to the non-believer weakening the Christian life of the believer.

If you find yourself thinking about whether you could marry a certain Christian man, do not only think about what he looks like or how clever he is. These are important things; but you will also need to ask yourself whether you are spiritually suited. Are you going to be able to strengthen each other's faith or will you tend to pull each other down spiritually? Do you agree about basic questions concerning your faith, such as how to understand the Bible and how you should worship God?

Marriage also involves the joining together of two families. What will your parents think about the possibility of marriage to this man?

Many things to think about for the future!

Always be careful to please God

Christian young people can easily fall into temptation when they go out by breaking God's command to keep sexual intimacy for marriage. It is important that you honour God and respect your boyfriend in this way. If your boyfriend encourages you to do things that are wrong before God, you must tell him what you think. If you really love each other and want to honour God, you must be prepared to wait for intimacy until you are married.

In our society, young people are being encouraged to think that it is alright to experience sexual intimacy with another person outside of marriage. You may be told that you will be missing out if you do not experience sexual intimacy outside marriage.

If you eat sweets that you have stolen, they might taste nice to you at the time. After a while the sweet taste goes and you are left feeling scared that your action might be discovered, as well as feeling guilty that you have done something wrong. Even though God has told us it is wrong, the experience of sexual intimacy can feel good at the time. Afterwards, however, you may recognise your mistake and sense that you have

offended God in what you have done. If you do not repent before God, it can cause you lasting spiritual damage.

At the present time in our society, more and more people are choosing to *live together* rather than get married. *Living together* is when a man and a woman share the same home and are sexually intimate with each other without making the commitment of marriage. This, too, is breaking God's commandment about sexual intimacy.

God's ways are always best

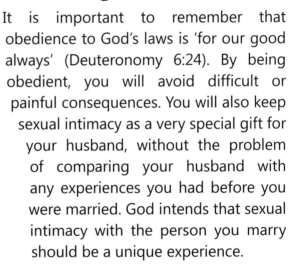

It is important to remember that obedience to God's laws is 'for our good always' (Deuteronomy 6:24). By being obedient, you will avoid difficult or painful consequences. You will also keep sexual intimacy as a very special gift for your husband, without the problem of comparing your husband with any experiences you had before you were married. God intends that sexual intimacy with the person you marry should be a unique experience.

Chapter 9
Preparing for the future

None of us knows exactly what the Lord plans for our life, but it may be that, after reading this book, you are quite looking forward to opportunities that will open up as you pass through puberty. You may even be looking forward to the possibility of having a family of your own at some point. The Bible encourages young men and women to consider this as a privilege.

So how can you prepare for the future? What qualities should you ask God to help you develop?

Diligence

'Whatever you do, work at it with all your heart, as working for the Lord, not for human masters, since you know that you will receive an inheritance from the Lord as a reward. It is the Lord Christ you are serving.' (Colossians 3:23-24 [NIV])

The above verse encourages us to be diligent. We have the very best of reasons – it pleases God who will reward us for our hard work.

Whatever God calls you to do in the future, whether in paid employment or as a volunteer, as a mother caring for family or in welcoming visitors, it is important to be diligent. A conscientious woman can be a constant source of encouragement and practical help to her family, the church and the wider community.

God's plan for many girls will be to marry and have a family, and formal education, though important, spends little time training you to prepare for this role. The Bible clearly encourages young women to consider this as a privilege. It explains that being a home-maker is part of a wife's role (Titus 2:5). In this important role, she supports her husband and looks after her children. Godly home-making requires resourcefulness and hard work (see Proverbs 31:15,16). Your knowledge and skills will be used by God to train up the next generation of men and women.

A submissive spirit

Wives are encouraged to be more concerned about having a gentle and non-argumentative spirit than about their outward appearance. These inner qualities are described as beautiful and are highly valued by God (1 Peter 3:4). If the Lord does plan for you to get married, you will need to have a willing spirit so that you can support your husband.

How can you learn to develop a submissive spirit? This is only done with God's help, since it goes against our natural pride and selfish ambition. The God-given way of developing such an attitude is to learn to submit to those that God has put in authority around you – your parents and your church leaders – and to submit to what God says in the Bible.

Modesty

As you pass through puberty, you will discover that it is possible to affect men by what you wear, what you do and what you say. Modesty is the desire of the heart to avoid stirring others to wrong sexual thoughts.

With regard to what you wear, one writer helpfully put immodest dress into three categories – too much (that is, dressing in a way that says 'look at me'), too little (that is, failing to cover up important parts that need special modesty) and too tight (clothing that reveals too much of the body shape).[3] Being modest should not stop you dressing prettily and looking beautiful.

---

3 'Too much, too little, too tight' by Robert G. Spinney published in the Free Grace Broadcaster No. 216 page 19.

It is helpful to remember that a modest attitude in your clothes and actions will, in itself, be very attractive to the right man.

Sexual purity

We live in a world where all kinds of influences can tempt a young woman away from the path that she knows will honour the Lord. You are warned, 'do not swerve to the right or to the left; turn your foot away from evil' (Proverbs 4:27).

Be careful to guard your emotions. Think carefully about what you read, watch and listen to. Romantic novels and films can be enjoyable; but they can encourage you to become emotionally involved in characters in stories, which may be unhelpful.

Be careful not to copy the lifestyle of ungodly friends who could tempt you to disobey God (Proverbs 1:10-18). Rather, choose faithful friends who will be willing to challenge you if you do something wrong or foolish (Proverbs 27:6).

The rewards of obedience are great!

The book of Proverbs teaches us that 'a woman who fears the Lord is to be praised' (Proverbs 31:30). She is to store up all the practical advice that she has read in the Bible so that if a time of testing and temptation comes along, she will be ready to act in the right way. If you are obedient, God promises to guide you in your decisions ('He shall direct your paths' Proverbs 3:6 [NKJV]).

Many young people are confused about how to live their lives, but with God's help you do not need to be. Many get damaged on the way, but if you follow God's ways and ask for God's help this need not happen. In the Bible, God promises to lead you and protect you in your life ('watching over the way of His saints' Proverbs 2:8).

As you seek to obey God in every area of your life, you will experience God's blessings in many ways. Life will not necessarily be free of troubles (Matthew 6:34), and you may not find the man of your dreams immediately! But God's word promises that you will know and experience God's goodness and be a blessing to others.